Faith *Notes*

Prayer &

Praise

Organizer

BARBOUR
PUBLISHING

Member of the
Evangelical Christian
Publishers Association

*Real prayer is life creating
and life changing.*
RICHARD FOSTER

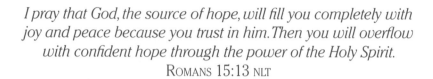

I pray that God, the source of hope, will fill you completely with joy and peace because you trust in him. Then you will overflow with confident hope through the power of the Holy Spirit.
Romans 15:13 NLT

Date and Time: 5/27/14 8:44 pm

Place: @ home in bed

Today, I prayed for: VBS, family

Prayer Requests: that Brandon truely enjoys over the road, that I get all volunteers for VBS, if I am to get a job, Brianna & Ethan at father's house, Bethany heading off to college

Answers to Prayer: the medicine is helping out, the van was fixed

Praises: put in time exercising

In the morning, O Lord, you hear my voice;
in the morning I lay my requests before you
and wait in expectation.
PSALM 5:3 NIV

Date and Time: ....

Place: ....

Today, I prayed for: ....

....

Prayer Requests: ....

....

....

....

....

....

....

....

....

....

Answers to Prayer:

Praises:

We constantly pray for you, that our God may
count you worthy of his calling,
and that by his power he may fulfill every good purpose of
yours and every act prompted by your faith.
2 THESSALONIANS 1:11 NIV

Date and Time: ....

Place: ....

Today, I prayed for: ....

....

Prayer Requests: ....

....

....

....

....

....

....

....

....

....

....

Answers to Prayer:

Praises:

Why are you downcast, O my soul?
Why so disturbed within me?
Put your hope in God, for I will yet praise him,
my Savior and my God.
PSALM 42:11 NIV

Date and Time: ....

Place: ....

Today, I prayed for: ....

....

Prayer Requests: ....

....

....

....

....

....

....

....

....

....

....

Answers to Prayer:

Praises:

Is any one of you in trouble?
He should pray. Is anyone happy?
Let him sing songs of praise.
JAMES 5:13 NIV

Date and Time: ....

Place: ....

Today, I prayed for: ....

....

Prayer Requests: ....

....

....

....

....

....

....

....

....

....

Answers to Prayer:

Praises:

*This is the confidence we have in approaching God:
that if we ask anything according to his will, he hears us.
And if we know that he hears us—whatever we ask—
we know that we have what we asked of him.*
1 John 5:14–15 NIV

Date and Time:

Place:

Today, I prayed for:

Prayer Requests:

Answers to Prayer:

Praises:

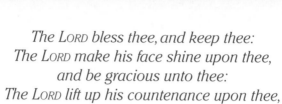

The LORD bless thee, and keep thee:
The LORD make his face shine upon thee,
and be gracious unto thee:
The LORD lift up his countenance upon thee,
and give thee peace.
NUMBERS 6:24–26 KJV

Date and Time:

Place:

Today, I prayed for:

Prayer Requests:

Answers to Prayer:

Praises:

I call on you, O God, for you will answer me;
give ear to me and hear my prayer.
PSALM 17:6 NIV

Date and Time: ....

Place: ....

Today, I prayed for: ....

....

Prayer Requests: ....

....

....

....

....

....

....

....

....

....

Answers to Prayer:

Praises:

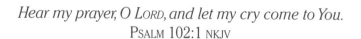

Hear my prayer, O Lord, and let my cry come to You.
PSALM 102:1 NKJV

Date and Time: ....

Place: ....

Today, I prayed for: ....

....

Prayer Requests: ....

....

....

....

....

....

....

....

....

....

....

Answers to Prayer:

Praises:

The Lord hath heard my supplication;
the Lord will receive my prayer.
PSALM 6:9 KJV

Date and Time: ....

Place: ....

Today, I prayed for: ....

....

Prayer Requests: ....

....

....

....

....

....

....

....

....

....

....

Answers to Prayer:

Praises:

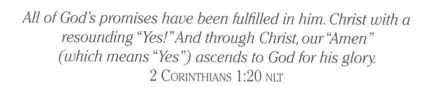

All of God's promises have been fulfilled in him. Christ with a resounding "Yes!" And through Christ, our "Amen" (which means "Yes") ascends to God for his glory.
2 Corinthians 1:20 NLT

Date and Time: ....

Place: ....

Today, I prayed for: ....

....

Prayer Requests: ....

....

....

....

....

....

....

....

....

....

Answers to Prayer:

Praises:

Pray in the Spirit at all times and on every occasion.
EPHESIANS 6:18 NLT

Date and Time: ....

Place: ....

Today, I prayed for: ....

....

Prayer Requests: ....

....

....

....

....

....

....

....

....

....

....

Answers to Prayer:

Praises:

*We are confident that he hears us
whenever we ask for anything that pleases him.
And since we know he hears us when we make our requests,
we also know that he will give us what we ask for.*
1 JOHN 5:14–15 NLT

Date and Time:

Place:

Today, I prayed for:

Prayer Requests:

Answers to Prayer:

Praises:

You faithfully answer our prayers with awesome deeds,
O God our savior.
PSALM 65:5 NLT

Date and Time: ....

Place: ....

Today, I prayed for: ....

....

Prayer Requests: ....

....

....

....

....

....

....

....

....

....

Answers to Prayer:

Praises:

Cast your burden on the Lord, and he will sustain you.
PSALM 55:22 NRSV

Date and Time: ....

Place: ....

Today, I prayed for: ....

....

Prayer Requests: ....

....

....

....

....

....

....

....

....

....

....

....

Answers to Prayer:

Praises:

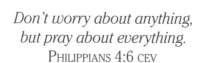

Don't worry about anything,
but pray about everything.
PHILIPPIANS 4:6 CEV

Date and Time: ....

Place: ....

Today, I prayed for: ....

....

Prayer Requests: ....

....

....

....

....

....

....

....

....

....

....

Answers to Prayer:

Praises:

Be joyful always; pray continually.
1 Thessalonians 5:16–17 NIV

Date and Time: ....

Place: ....

Today, I prayed for: ....

....

Prayer Requests: ....

....

....

....

....

....

....

....

....

....

Answers to Prayer:

Praises:

You are near to everyone whose prayers are sincere.
PSALM 145:18 CEV

Date and Time: ....

Place: ....

Today, I prayed for: ....

....

Prayer Requests: ....

....

....

....

....

....

....

....

....

....

....

Answers to Prayer:

Praises:

O Lord, you are my God;
I will exalt you and praise your name,
for in perfect faithfulness
you have done marvelous things,
things planned long ago.
Isaiah 25:1 niv

Date and Time:

Place:

Today, I prayed for:

Prayer Requests:

Answers to Prayer:

Praises:

*"You are worthy, our Lord and God,
to receive glory and honor and power,
for you created all things,
and by your will they were created
and have their being."*
REVELATION 4:11 NIV

Date and Time: ....

Place: ....

Today, I prayed for: ....

....

Prayer Requests: ....

....

....

....

....

....

....

....

....

....

....

Answers to Prayer:

Praises:

*May your unfailing love rest upon us, O Lord,
even as we put our hope in you.*
Psalm 33:22 NIV

Date and Time: ....

Place: ....

Today, I prayed for: ....

....

Prayer Requests: ....

....

....

....

....

....

....

....

....

....

Answers to Prayer:

Praises:

LORD, God of Israel, there is no God like you in heaven above or on earth below—you who keep your covenant of love with your servants who continue wholeheartedly in your way.
1 KINGS 8:23 NIV

Date and Time: ....

Place: ....

Today, I prayed for: ....

....

Prayer Requests: ....

....

....

....

....

....

....

....

....

....

Answers to Prayer:

Praises:

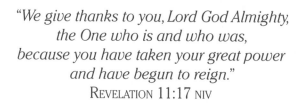

"We give thanks to you, Lord God Almighty,
the One who is and who was,
because you have taken your great power
and have begun to reign."
REVELATION 11:17 NIV

Date and Time: ....

Place: ....

Today, I prayed for: ....

....

Prayer Requests: ....

....

....

....

....

....

....

....

....

....

....

Answers to Prayer:

Praises:

Let the morning bring me word of your unfailing love,
for I have put my trust in you.
Show me the way I should go,
for to you I lift up my soul.
PSALM 143:8 NIV

Date and Time: ....

Place: ....

Today, I prayed for: ....

....

Prayer Requests: ....

....

....

....

....

....

....

....

....

....

....

Answers to Prayer:

Praises:

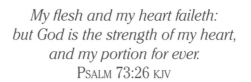

My flesh and my heart faileth:
but God is the strength of my heart,
and my portion for ever.
Psalm 73:26 KJV

Date and Time: ....

Place: ....

Today, I prayed for: ....

....

Prayer Requests: ....

....

....

....

....

....

....

....

....

....

....

Answers to Prayer:

Praises:

Show me your ways, O LORD, teach me your paths;
guide me in your truth and teach me,
for you are God my Savior,
and my hope is in you all day long.
PSALM 25:4–5 NIV

Date and Time: ....

Place: ....

Today, I prayed for: ....

....

Prayer Requests: ....

....

....

....

....

....

....

....

....

....

....

....

....

Answers to Prayer:

Praises:

The LORD…hears the prayer of the righteous.
PROVERBS 15:29 NRSV

Date and Time: ....

Place: ....

Today, I prayed for: ....

....

Prayer Requests: ....

....

....

....

....

....

....

....

....

....

....

Answers to Prayer:

Praises:

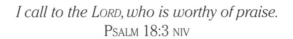

I call to the LORD, who is worthy of praise.
PSALM 18:3 NIV

Date and Time: ....

Place: ....

Today, I prayed for: ....

....

Prayer Requests: ....

....

....

....

....

....

....

....

....

....

....

Answers to Prayer:

Praises:

Hear my voice in accordance with your love;
preserve my life, O LORD, according to your laws.
PSALM 119:149 NIV

Date and Time: ....

Place: ....

Today, I prayed for: ....

....

Prayer Requests: ....

....

....

....

....

....

....

....

....

....

....

Answers to Prayer:

Praises:

I will praise you, O LORD, among the nations;
I will sing praises to your name.
2 SAMUEL 22:50 NIV

Date and Time: ....

Place: ....

Today, I prayed for: ....

....

Prayer Requests: ....

....

....

....

....

....

....

....

....

....

Answers to Prayer:

Praises:

The prayer of the righteous is powerful and effective.
JAMES 5:16 NRSV

Date and Time: ....

Place: ....

Today, I prayed for: ....

....

Prayer Requests: ....

....

....

....

....

....

....

....

....

....

....

Answers to Prayer:

Praises:

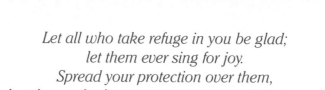

Let all who take refuge in you be glad;
let them ever sing for joy.
Spread your protection over them,
that those who love your name may rejoice in you.
PSALM 5:11 NIV

Date and Time: ....

Place: ....

Today, I prayed for: ....

....

Prayer Requests: ....

....

....

....

....

....

....

....

....

....

Answers to Prayer:

Praises:

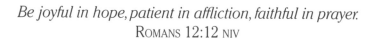

Be joyful in hope, patient in affliction, faithful in prayer.
ROMANS 12:12 NIV

Date and Time: ....

Place: ....

Today, I prayed for: ....

....

Prayer Requests: ....

....

....

....

....

....

....

....

....

....

....

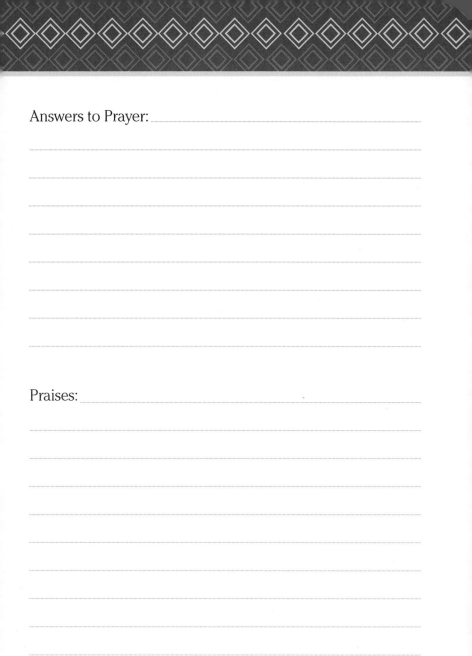

Answers to Prayer:

Praises:

I will praise you, O LORD, with all my heart;
I will tell of all your wonders.
I will be glad and rejoice in you;
I will sing praise to your name, O Most High.
PSALM 9:1–2 NIV

Date and Time:

Place:

Today, I prayed for:

Prayer Requests:

Answers to Prayer:

_____

_____

_____

_____

_____

Praises:

_____

_____

_____

_____

_____

_____

_____

_____

_____

Your ways, O God, are holy. What god is so great as our God?
You are the God who performs miracles;
you display your power among the peoples.
PSALM 77:13–14 NIV

Date and Time: ....

Place: ....

Today, I prayed for: ....

....

Prayer Requests: ....

....

....

....

....

....

....

....

....

....

Answers to Prayer:

Praises:

*Answer me, O L*ORD, *out of the goodness of your love;*
in your great mercy turn to me.
PSALM 69:16 NIV

Date and Time: ....

Place: ....

Today, I prayed for: ....

....

Prayer Requests: ....

....

....

....

....

....

....

....

....

Answers to Prayer:

Praises:

We give thanks to God and the Father of our Lord Jesus Christ, praying always for you.
COLOSSIANS 1:3 KJV

Date and Time: ....

Place: ....

Today, I prayed for: ....

....

Prayer Requests: ....

....

....

....

....

....

....

....

....

....

Answers to Prayer:

Praises:

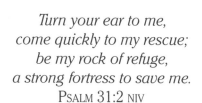

Turn your ear to me,
come quickly to my rescue;
be my rock of refuge,
a strong fortress to save me.
PSALM 31:2 NIV

Date and Time:

Place:

Today, I prayed for:

Prayer Requests:

Answers to Prayer:

Praises:

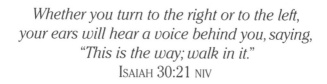

Whether you turn to the right or to the left,
your ears will hear a voice behind you, saying,
"This is the way; walk in it."
ISAIAH 30:21 NIV

Date and Time: ....

Place: ....

Today, I prayed for: ....

....

Prayer Requests: ....

....

....

....

....

....

....

....

....

....

Answers to Prayer:

Praises:

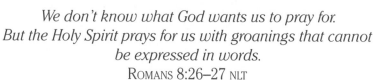

We don't know what God wants us to pray for.
But the Holy Spirit prays for us with groanings that cannot
be expressed in words.
ROMANS 8:26–27 NLT

Date and Time:

Place:

Today, I prayed for:

Prayer Requests:

Answers to Prayer:

Praises:

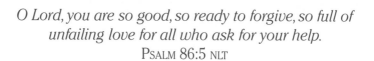

O Lord, you are so good, so ready to forgive, so full of unfailing love for all who ask for your help.
PSALM 86:5 NLT

Date and Time: ....

Place: ....

Today, I prayed for: ....

....

Prayer Requests: ....

....

....

....

....

....

....

....

....

....

....

Answers to Prayer:

Praises:

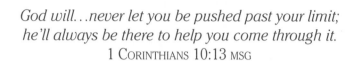

God will…never let you be pushed past your limit;
he'll always be there to help you come through it.
1 Corinthians 10:13 msg

Date and Time: ....

Place: ....

Today, I prayed for: ....

....

Prayer Requests: ....

....

....

....

....

....

....

....

....

....

....

Answers to Prayer:

Praises:

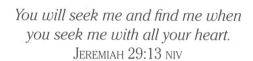

*You will seek me and find me when
you seek me with all your heart.*
JEREMIAH 29:13 NIV

Date and Time: ....

Place: ....

Today, I prayed for: ....

....

Prayer Requests: ....

....

....

....

....

....

....

....

....

....

....

Answers to Prayer:

Praises:

If you confess with your mouth, "Jesus is Lord,"
and believe in your heart that God raised him from the dead,
you will be saved.
ROMANS 10:9 NIV

Date and Time: ....

Place: ....

Today, I prayed for: ....

....

Prayer Requests: ....

....

....

....

....

....

....

....

....

....

Answers to Prayer:

Praises:

Listen to my prayer, O God,
do not ignore my plea.
PSALM 55:1 NIV

Date and Time: ....

Place: ....

Today, I prayed for: ....

....

Prayer Requests: ....

....

....

....

....

....

....

....

....

....

Answers to Prayer:

Praises:

Oh, that their hearts would be inclined to fear me and keep all my commands always, so that it might go well with them and their children forever!
DEUTERONOMY 5:29 NIV

Date and Time:

Place:

Today, I prayed for:

Prayer Requests:

Answers to Prayer:

Praises:

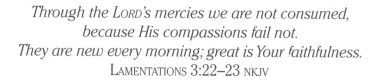

Through the LORD's mercies we are not consumed,
because His compassions fail not.
They are new every morning; great is Your faithfulness.
LAMENTATIONS 3:22–23 NKJV

Date and Time: ....

Place: ....

Today, I prayed for: ....

....

Prayer Requests: ....

....

....

....

....

....

....

....

....

....

Answers to Prayer:

Praises:

His ears are open to their prayers.
1 PETER 3:12 NLT

Date and Time:

Place:

Today, I prayed for:

Prayer Requests:

Answers to Prayer:

Praises:

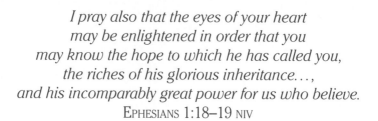

*I pray also that the eyes of your heart
may be enlightened in order that you
may know the hope to which he has called you,
the riches of his glorious inheritance...,
and his incomparably great power for us who believe.*
EPHESIANS 1:18–19 NIV

Date and Time: ....

Place: ....

Today, I prayed for: ....

....

Prayer Requests: ....

....

....

....

....

....

....

....

....

....

....

Answers to Prayer:

Praises:

God says to you, "My grace is all you need."
2 Corinthians 12:9 tev

Date and Time: ....

Place: ....

Today, I prayed for: ....

....

Prayer Requests: ....

....

....

....

....

....

....

....

....

....

Answers to Prayer:

Praises:

But now thus says the LORD, he who created you…
he who formed you.…
Do not fear, for I have redeemed you;
I have called you by name, you are mine.
ISAIAH 43:1 NRSV

Date and Time: ....

Place: ....

Today, I prayed for: ....

....

Prayer Requests: ....

....

....

....

....

....

....

....

....

....

....

Answers to Prayer:

Praises:

"But when you pray, go into your room, close the door and pray to your Father, who is unseen. Then your Father, who sees what is done in secret, will reward you."
MATTHEW 6:6 NIV

Date and Time: ....

Place: ....

Today, I prayed for: ....

....

Prayer Requests: ....

....

....

....

....

....

....

....

....

....

Answers to Prayer:

Praises:

"Yet not my will, but yours be done."
LUKE 22:42 NIV

Date and Time:

Place:

Today, I prayed for:

Prayer Requests:

Answers to Prayer:

Praises:

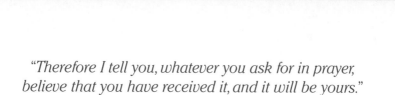

"Therefore I tell you, whatever you ask for in prayer,
believe that you have received it, and it will be yours."
MARK 11:24 NIV

Date and Time: ....

Place: ....

Today, I prayed for: ....

....

Prayer Requests: ....

....

....

....

....

....

....

....

....

....

Answers to Prayer:

Praises:

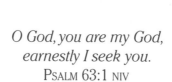

O God, you are my God,
earnestly I seek you.
PSALM 63:1 NIV

Date and Time: ....

Place: ....

Today, I prayed for: ....

....

Prayer Requests: ....

....

....

....

....

....

....

....

....

....

Answers to Prayer:

Praises:

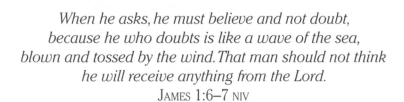

When he asks, he must believe and not doubt,
because he who doubts is like a wave of the sea,
blown and tossed by the wind. That man should not think
he will receive anything from the Lord.
JAMES 1:6–7 NIV

Date and Time: ....

Place: ....

Today, I prayed for: ....

....

Prayer Requests: ....

....

....

....

....

....

....

....

....

....

....

Answers to Prayer:

Praises:

You need to persevere so that when you have done the will of God, you will receive what he has promised.
HEBREWS 10:36 NIV

Date and Time: ....

Place: ....

Today, I prayed for: ....

....

Prayer Requests: ....

....

....

....

....

....

....

....

....

....

Answers to Prayer:

Praises:

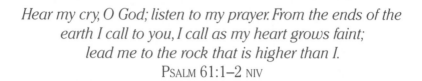

Hear my cry, O God; listen to my prayer. From the ends of the earth I call to you, I call as my heart grows faint; lead me to the rock that is higher than I.
PSALM 61:1–2 NIV

Date and Time: ....

Place: ....

Today, I prayed for: ....

....

Prayer Requests: ....

....

....

....

....

....

....

....

....

....

....

Answers to Prayer:

Praises:

Be still before the LORD and wait patiently for him.
PSALM 37:7 NIV

Date and Time: ....

Place: ....

Today, I prayed for: ....

....

Prayer Requests: ....

....

....

....

....

....

....

....

....

....

....

....

Answers to Prayer:

Praises:

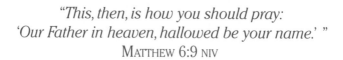

"This, then, is how you should pray:
'Our Father in heaven, hallowed be your name.' "
MATTHEW 6:9 NIV

Date and Time: ....

Place: ....

Today, I prayed for: ....

....

Prayer Requests: ....

....

....

....

....

....

....

....

....

....

....

....

Answers to Prayer:

Praises:

They that wait upon the Lord shall renew their strength.
They shall mount up with wings like eagles;
they shall run and not be weary;
they shall walk and not faint.
ISAIAH 40:31 TLB

Date and Time: ....

Place: ....

Today, I prayed for: ....

....

Prayer Requests: ....

....

....

....

....

....

....

....

....

....

....

Answers to Prayer:

Praises:

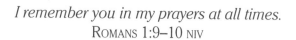

I remember you in my prayers at all times.
Romans 1:9–10 niv

Date and Time: ....

Place: ....

Today, I prayed for: ....

....

Prayer Requests: ....

....

....

....

....

....

....

....

....

....

....

Answers to Prayer:

_____

_____

_____

_____

_____

_____

Praises:

_____

_____

_____

_____

_____

_____

_____

_____

_____

_____

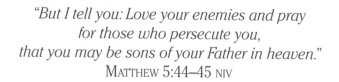

*"But I tell you: Love your enemies and pray
for those who persecute you,
that you may be sons of your Father in heaven."*
MATTHEW 5:44–45 NIV

Date and Time: ....

Place: ....

Today, I prayed for: ....

....

Prayer Requests: ....

....

....

....

....

....

....

....

....

....

Answers to Prayer:

Praises:

God…delights in genuine prayers.
PROVERBS 15:8 MSG

Date and Time: ....

Place: ....

Today, I prayed for: ....

....

Prayer Requests: ....

....

....

....

....

....

....

....

....

....

....

Answers to Prayer:

Praises:

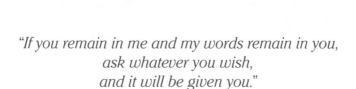

*"If you remain in me and my words remain in you,
ask whatever you wish,
and it will be given you."*
JOHN 15:7 NIV

Date and Time: ....

Place: ....

Today, I prayed for: ....

....

Prayer Requests: ....

....

....

....

....

....

....

....

....

....

Answers to Prayer:

Praises:

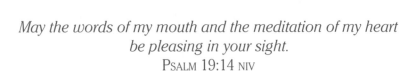

May the words of my mouth and the meditation of my heart be pleasing in your sight.
PSALM 19:14 NIV

Date and Time:

Place:

Today, I prayed for:

Prayer Requests:

Answers to Prayer:

Praises:

"If my people who are called by my name, will humble themselves and pray and seek my face and turn from their wicked ways, then will I hear from heaven and will forgive their sin and will heal their land."
2 CHRONICLES 7:14 NIV

Date and Time: ....

Place: ....

Today, I prayed for: ....

....

....

Prayer Requests: ....

....

....

....

....

....

....

....

....

....

....

Answers to Prayer:

Praises:

"Lord, teach us to pray."
LUKE 11:1 NIV

Date and Time: ....

Place: ....

Today, I prayed for: ....

....

Prayer Requests: ....

....

....

....

....

....

....

....

....

....

Answers to Prayer:

Praises:

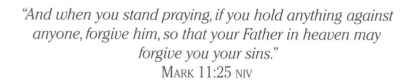

"And when you stand praying, if you hold anything against anyone, forgive him, so that your Father in heaven may forgive you your sins."
MARK 11:25 NIV

Date and Time: ....

Place: ....

Today, I prayed for: ....

....

Prayer Requests: ....

....

....

....

....

....

....

....

....

....

....

....

Answers to Prayer:

Praises:

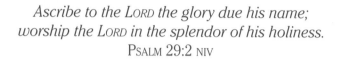

*Ascribe to the L*ORD *the glory due his name;*
*worship the L*ORD *in the splendor of his holiness.*
PSALM 29:2 NIV

Date and Time: ....

Place: ....

Today, I prayed for: ....

....

Prayer Requests: ....

....

....

....

....

....

....

....

....

....

....

Answers to Prayer:

Praises: